SNOW
FLAKES

Commentary on the Book

From small beginnings come great things. Aryaman proves this in his rhythmical and ingeniously rhymed verses, baring no obvious literary mark of immaturity. More than a glimpse of what we call 'poetry' in his instinct for metaphor and memorable phrasing. Utterly different from the juvenile poetry that one would come to expect from a young boy.

My sincere and humble appreciation for his launching the charitable foundation called Little Planet to help wildlife and nature conservation. Would [wish] that more youth follow this path.

—**Amitabh Bachchan**

In the rush to hang on to the gravy train some things of great importance get left behind on the platform—such as respect for language, cultural affinities, artistic pursuit. It is therefore noteworthy that young Aryaman chooses to stand apart and align himself to the world of letters. His first book of poetry *Snowflakes* shows promise of a bright future ahead.

—**Javed Akhtar**

Aryaman's poems are a reflection of his vast wisdom and values at such a young age. The depth in his poetry covering various aspects of life moved me. I am proud of Aryaman and wish him all the success in life.

—**Kailash Satyarthi**

Writing your first book is always special, signifying an unadulterated first voice. It is the time when a writer decides to share with the world what till now was purely a personal journey. Aryaman's poetry is a honest search which bravely examines every emotion he encounters and looks into the eyes of the familiar and the not so familiar emotions with the same intensity.

—**Prasoon Joshi**

SNOW FLAKES
A Collection of Poems

ARYAMAN DARDA

RUPA

Published by
Rupa Publications India Pvt. Ltd 2019
7/16, Ansari Road, Daryaganj
New Delhi 110002

Sales centres:
Allahabad Bengaluru Chennai
Hyderabad Jaipur Kathmandu
Kolkata Mumbai

Copyright © Aryaman Darda, Little Planet Foundation 2019
Book design: Mugdha Sadhwani
Illustrations: Prabhjyot Majithia

This is a work of fiction. Names, characters, places and incidents are either the product of the author's imagination or are used fictitiously and any resemblance to any actual person, living or dead, events or
locales is entirely coincidental.

All rights reserved.

No part of this publication may be reproduced, transmitted, or stored in a retrieval system, in any form or by any means, electronic, mechanical, photocopying, recording or otherwise, without the prior permission of the publisher.

ISBN: 978-93-5333-339-3

First impression 2019

10 9 8 7 6 5 4 3 2 1

The moral right of the author has been asserted.

This book is sold subject to the condition that it shall not, by way of trade or otherwise, be lent, resold, hired out, or otherwise circulated, without the publisher's prior consent, in any form of binding or
cover other than that in which it is published.

Aryaman, a bright young man
on the threshold of youth, has a
deep interest in wildlife since early
childhood. In 2017, he launched
'Little Planet Foundation'
(www.littleplanetfoundation.org),
a non-profit initiative to make
a difference to our wildlife and nature.
An avid photographer, Aryaman held
his maiden photography exhibition
in Mumbai the same year.

In addition to the above, Aryaman
is interested in physics, mathematics,
football, skiing, and diving to catch
a glimpse of the underwater world.

Aryaman has been an avid reader
of both both fiction and non-
fiction from an early age. He enjoys
expressing his thoughts and feelings
in poetry, as this comes naturally
to him. He wrote his first poem
at the age of 10, which is part of
this collection.

There is a humming bird and a cow, a busy bazaar and a walk on the beach, a delicious breakfast and a few snowflakes. Aryaman Darda brings poetry to everyday life and humdrum objects, perceptively imagining and recreating things.

The poems included in this volume are curated to take you from the realm of real life to a life of fantasy, and then bring you back, wiser from the experience.

Written with the enthusiasm of a young heart and the perception of an observant mind, Aryaman Darda's poems will leave you wanting for more.

Turn the pages, read on and be engulfed by *Snowflakes*!

Contents

Hummingbird / 1

Who Am I? / 2

Busy Bazaar / 3

Rain / 5

The Mountain / 6

The Silent Alley / 8

The Downside of Being an Achiever / 11

A Delicious Breakfast / 13

The Super-jumping Cow! / 15

A Walk on the Beach / 17

My Mother, My Angel / 19

The Forest / 20

To Watch the Sky / 21

Love / 23

Dedication / 24

What Lies Within! / 25

Ode to a Clock / 27

Brown Man's Burden / 28

Nervous / 31

Never Judge a Book by its Cover / 32

The Power to Kill One's Passion / 33

Just a Smile / 35

Never Quit / 36

Away / 37

Blue / 39

Eternally Strive / 41

The Long Walk / 43

What? / 45

The Outsider / 46

The Power of Letting Go / 49

Snowflake / 51

Wait / 53

Into the Wild / 55

Figure it Out / 57

Time / 58

Dream / 61

The Soulful Woman / 63

Gratitude Concealed / 65

My Melodious Guitar / 67

My Treasured Grandmother / 69

In Vain / 71

Mystical Tree / 73

A Beautiful Day / 75

The Road Ahead / 76

The Great Artist / 79

Hummingbird

Hummingbird, O hummingbird!
What does your hum signify?
Hummingbird, O hummingbird!
O please, elucidate why?
You hum melodiously in the morning and in
the wee hours at night,
You don't seem to stop yourself till the clouds go by.

You are feeble and so small,
And yet recognized by us all.
Hummingbird, O hummingbird!
Do the others bustle you?
Hummingbird, O hummingbird!
Or is it that you torment them too?

Hummingbird, O hummingbird!
There are incessant questions I wish to ask you,
So will you take some time out and come tomorrow soon?

Who Am I?

Who am I? I always tend to wonder.
Am I just a flower or a pod,
Blooming in the season of spring?
Or a bubble bursting in a wink,
After its life is over?

I always tend to wonder.
Do I have a goal or a task,
Like the buzzing bees collecting the sweet nectar?
Or just a person wearing a mask,
Cast away in the shadows,
Of a dark, cloudy weather?
Or am I a wealthy famous man,
Doing everything that I simply can?

I often tend to wonder, who am I?
So, do you know who you are?
It is time you know, you are somebody too.

Busy Bazaar

A bright Sunday morning, on reaching the bazaar, I found
that there were people around, more than I could count.
Maidens grinding sandalwood, henna and spice,
Vendor on the scale, weighing saffron, lentils and rice.

Grocers selling juicy lemons, pomegranates and plums,
Musicians melodiously playing bansuri, sitar and drums.
There was an abundance of wheat, corn and barley seeds,
There were elegant necklaces of varied shaped beads.

All around, I spotted rows of countless jars,
Containing a variety of wonderful and fragrant dry flowers.
The bazaar was full of endless crowds and items to see,
I finally left the bazaar in excitement and glee.

Rain

Pitter, patter,
It comes down!
Scatter, splatter,
It comes down!

Down in heaps,
Slowly it creeps
Forward in an elegant motion,
It simply mesmerizes us!
Like a mirage in the scorching desert,
People stare, stare and care
As it comes gushing down,
Making a booming yet tranquil sound!

The rain, the clouds, the thunder, the lightning!
Goodness gracious, it can become quite frightening!
Yet, as I look out,
Out of the big window,
I think about the winsome rain,
And how it might fall down with plenty of pain.

Pitter, patter,
It comes down!
Scatter, splatter,
It comes down!

The Mountain

This mountain, so gigantic,
With its glistening peak.
And its withered body,
Breaking away as time passes.
This mountain too,
Has to move on,
For everybody, the time comes.
This mountain has witnessed red-letter days!
And it might not see it again.
The mountain is the final challenge,
The hardest challenge in day-to-day lives.
The mountain has undergone pain, grief and sorrow,
Yet it thrives in this abundant habitat.

The mountain is the challenge,
For if we climb the mountain,
Great fame will be showered upon us.
It is us who will thrive in this glorious world,
It is us who will revolutionize history!

If only we can climb the mountain.

Don't you see?
We are the mountain!
We face our own challenges!
We deal with pain, grief and sorrow!
We climb to the highest of our ability!
For it is we who have to witness great things!

This is all because we have climbed the mountain,
And we will continue climbing this mountain...
LIFE!

The Silent Alley

It's so dark, so eerie,
The cobblestone path.
Street lights flickering,
It's so deserted, so full of mysteries.
I feel it when walking down the alley.

A chill runs down my spine,
My heart is beating faster.
Sweat slowly trickles down my forehead,
I walk with suspicion.
Looking over my shoulder and from side to side,
My sixth sense takes over,
Fear now rules.
Someone is following me in the shadows,
With eyes as dark as the night.
My eyebrows furrow,
And me, well, I run.

Knowing it is time,
Knowing the stop sign is approaching,
I stop!
A fall to the ground with a loud thump,
Skin, colourless, face, expressionless.
And then, the shadow emerges,
From behind my crumpled body.
It laughs a long laugh and is never seen again.

It's so dark, so eerie,
The cobblestone path.
Street lights flickering,
It's so deserted, so full of mysteries.
I feel it when walking down the alley.

The Downside of Being an Achiever

Who is an achiever?
A person who has found the solution to a problem
Or has simply just done something creditable?

There are many achievers in this great world,
And if you look at them,
You won't find them interesting just one bit.

Fame and fortune is showered upon them,
They have it all, everything they could ever ask for.
They work hard every day and rest at night,
They will charge upon a problem with all their might.
Victorious they will be when they have achieved.

They are happy, they are content, but are they really so?
Do they really have it all?
Deep inside that smile,
Lies a frown waiting to come out.

Popularity is a vicious cycle,
Which has no end.
Fame is like drugs,
Which is terribly addictive!

An achiever can have everything,
Yet feel like he has nothing!

His heart craves for freedom and friends,
And his brain wants to follow the new trends.

He has no choice but to be glued to the desk,
Typing like a lunatic on that interactive computer.
Wishing he was like any ordinary person,
Wishing he had nothing at all.
Except that little sliver of freedom,
Everybody deserves.
He arises from his chair and goes out into the balcony,
Spectating the marvellous sunset
And thinking he has one day less to live.

A Delicious Breakfast

The fork enters my mouth,
The luscious blueberry juice squirting out of the crepe,
Trickles down my lips
as I eat the crepe, with satisfaction.

The sumptuous taste of the crepe
is one beyond compare.
The frothy white cream
stains the sides of my lips,
As I chew the beautifully cooked crepe in bliss.

The golden caramel on top of the crepe
is cooked to perfection.
It is sweet yet bitter in taste,
It leaves me in a state of paradise.
The strawberries crowning the top
are looking thoroughly themselves.

The pink transforms my tongue,
As I chew the beautiful crepe in bliss.
The brown yet rich complexity of the crepe
is a sight in itself!

Forget the pyramids, the Eiffel Tower or
the Leaning Tower of Pisa,
Instead eat the yellow cheese—ah!
No dish compares to this,
As I chew this beautiful crepe in bliss!

The Super-jumping Cow!

I'll tell you the story of a super-jumping cow,
When she jumped, everyone would go, 'Wow'!
She jumped all day and jumped all night,
She jumped till she was out of sight.
She was heavy, fat and tall,
She rarely ever had a fall.
She always challenged herself,
Saying that she was no elf,
But after all, she was the super-jumping cow.

She was seldom tired or ill,
She kept jumping and was never fulfilled.
She acted in plays and jumped in shows,
People came to see her, rows after rows.
She became ridiculously rich,
But little did she know, there was a hitch!
Her master would say that she was really funny,
But instead of paying the super-jumping cow,
They paid him money!

One day, she decided to present,
Something to the people that they would not resent.
She decided to jump right over the moon,
But her life was to end soon.

She stretched her muscles,
And checked her springing legs.
And with one mighty leap,
She jumped real steep.
She left earth and was over the moon!

But she could not come back,
For space had different plans!
There was no gravity in space,
You should have seen the look on the
super-jumping cow's face!
She was floating in mid-air,
From earth she looked bright and fair.
She was seen all over the world, even in Spain!
But alas, the super-jumping cow was never seen again.

A Walk on the Beach

The sun was setting over the infinite horizon line,
I was magnetized by that sight so fine.
Slender golden rays were emitting from the sun,
I realized I had no regrets—none.

Walking peacefully by the shore,
I felt like I was knocking on heaven's door.
The waves were approaching with a speed great yet tender,
The dark blue waters made me want to go into slumber.

It was serene and tranquil at dusk,
There was a fragrance in the air, that of musk.
As I walked on the sand,
The whole tableau looked quite grand.

The last few gorgeous rays of the vibrant sun had disappeared,
And yet again, the moon had instantly reappeared.
The luminescence of the moon had lit most,
The silver sea and the silver coast.

I fancied walking across the beach,
But I knew I had many lessons to teach.
I set foot in my car and drove away,
Knowing that I would definitely come back here one day.

My Mother, My Angel

I walk in after a rough day, tired from school,
I see her smile, she sits on her favourite couch.
Conversing on the phone, I think to myself,
How would my life be without her?

The sight of seeing her beautiful face with each passing day
is a sign of assurance and comfort which is there to stay.
For mothers are the ones who have brought us into this world,
Who endlessly shower us with their infinite adoration and love.

I love and appreciate my mother beyond compare,
For her big heart which only knows how to care.
She does not only see me for me,
But for who I am—and could possibly be.

My mother time and again comforts me with her warm hug,
And tells me, 'I am always proud of you'—with a snug.
Sure she can be a little persuasive and assertive,
And we get into a squabble time and again,
But eventually, it's all for my benefit and utmost gain.

I would rarely agree with my mother's parenting strategies,
But definitely on the fact that she alone knows my prodigy.
I admire and respect her from the bottom of my heart,
For I know, when I cross the finish line after a fresh start,
She alone will applaud with all her heart.

The Forest

A dense forest of the west,
The shimmering light of the moon on its crest.
The rustling leaves hum a song of joy,
The wind handles them like toys.

The redwoods look healthy and fit,
On the dirt, their stumps sit.
For everything they have found,
Growing old and sleeping sound.

The birds are chirping on the trees,
I listen as I sit down on my knees.
The forest around me is so vast,
It has been through the funny present to the bitter past.

And as I sit, I remember the redwoods that stood
with their thick branches and huge hood.
They are watching me with their keen sight,
Knowing that they are in a plight.

For out come those heartless men,
Who kill the trees in great numbers yet again.
We must save these natural wonders,
Saving the wild from the aggressive hunters.

To Watch the Sky

The crystal blue sky,
The white doves are flying high.
Serenity rings,
Like the nature's melodious hymns.

The sun rises up so strong,
Yet keeping the sky blue and warm.
The cool breeze carves its way through,
Translucent just like the sparkling dew.

Standing below, watching like a spectator,
Admiring this beautiful creation.
The crystal blue sky,
Always seems so mighty and high.

Love

Compassion flows through you,
Your brain and your soul.
Love is a tranquil experience,
Like sitting under a silent tree.

Beside a free-flowing stream,
Below the radiant yellow sun.
Love provides warmth to our body,
Warmth like no other feeling.

A security that can enchant us in the most chilling times,
Warmth that can bring back the most pleasant memories.
Passion cannot be touched but only felt,
From the vigorous roars of the lion to the soft touch of velvet.

Love emanates from each one of us,
And we thrive and survive on it.
Love tells us that we have a reason to live,
And live just to find out that reason.

Love and compassion is pure and unforgotten,
We show it knowingly, and seldom unknowingly,
In the purest of forms,
Yet it remains hidden in our deepest void.

Love is a bright light that creates an instant spark within all of us.
Love is pure,
Love is youthful,
Love is eternal,
Love is forever.

Dedication

There is the final moment in life that defines who you are,
A long and treacherous journey taken so far.

You walk and walk down that crowded lane,
Where lies a body, engulfed in flames.

People wear white on this despondent day,
The sky encounters all the fifty shades of grey.

We recite aloud the ceremonial goodbye,
The ashes camouflage with the ground and the soul rises to the clouded blue sky.

That time when tears come streaming down,
And the people bring out their miserable frowns.

The moment when your dedication shows,
You get reassured as a new life grows.

You may plead with guilt on your face,
But the biggest challenge is letting your loved ones go.

What Lies Within!

Ever thought of going near the sun?
From afar, he looks like a gentle ball of light.
But within, he is a fiery sphere with ego and jealousy.
A heap of ferocity and rage is ready to escape,
From his circular shape.

The sun provides us with heat and warmth,
He is the light to our darkness.
But deep within, he is troubled!
Inner conflict baffles him.
We do not know what lies within,
For he is unpredictable.

The sun's vast outstretched reach
Is what is keeping us intact.
You see, he cares for us, this sun.
But can we really trust him?
For one day with the help of Ares,
He will unleash his mighty wrath,
On all his little followers!

The inner emotions will come exploding out!
So, do we really know our sun well?
Can we predict the actions of our ancient friend?
We cannot!
For we do not possess
the answer that lies within.

Ode to a Clock

Clock, you are a graceful runner
who never stops, and never sleeps.
Your face is nothing but informative,
And your features are crystal clear.
Your hands encompass the world,
Exhibiting time as it is.

The intricacy of your mechanism
shows how deep your heart lies.
You are the guardian of time itself
and a wake-up call for many.
Clock, you are as historic as the sands of time themselves,
And an everlasting masterpiece.

I admire you, O clock,
For you make me follow a routine,
You teach us to forget the past
and work our way towards a triumphant tomorrow.
You are realistic and display time just like the truth.
For you, time neither flies nor stops,
That being the essence of your existence.

O clock, you are as old as any mountain,
Thereby, you have witnessed a lot of history.
But you are the only one who knows and believes,
That time is still a complete mystery.

Brown Man's Burden

The sweat, the blood, the agony,
It was never enough.
All the indigo, rich spices and pearls,
They too were not enough.

Right from the East to the West,
And from the North to the South,
The oppression of the age's yolk screeched in India.
Are we slaves?
To work tirelessly for the British and to be called their trinkets.
Are we slaves?

That they took away what was rightfully ours,
Like confident tricksters?
You said you would mitigate our illiteracy,
But we were blindfolded and foolish enough to believe you.

Then after the wrath of the Titans,
You violently destroyed our Olympus.
We were just a showpiece in your collection of colonies,
You made us the puppets of your intricate play.

Our freedom diminished like the light through a dark tunnel,
With time you stole away our rich Indian culture.
The hours of labour were not enough to satisfy,
Even the smallest part of you.

We were not allowed to pursue any of our fancies,
All the clubs made sure of that.
You considered us stray dogs,
And we were unwelcome everywhere.
The scary sight of seeing our families being taken away,
And to make them helpless peasants.

We never got the opportunity to rise then,
But we eventually did after years of non-violent wars.
We proved to be better people.

But remember, before the urbanization,
Before the industrialization,
Before the restoration of wealth,
And before the striking yet elegant beauty,
Each one of us had to bear the brown man's burden.

Nervous

Violently shaking my legs,
Irritatingly twitching my eyes.
Indecisively pointing my fingers around the room,
Angrily banging my forehead against my hands.

Restlessly grinding my teeth,
Roughly biting my long nails.
Anxiously feeling my heart,
Cautiously breathing unevenly.

Slowly manoeuvring my eyes around the area,
Silently uttering loud expletives.
Spontaneously sweating through my skin,
Consciously undoing my hair.

Furiously rotating my ankles,
Mysteriously rolling my eyes.
Sporadically chewing on my tongue,
Defectively cracking the bones in my thumb.

Unsuccessfully comprehending the replies,
And nervously chewing my boss's brains.
Nervously hoping for the best,
Nervously answering her questions.

Nervously reviewing my options,
Nervously grabbing my opportunities.
Nervously exiting the room,
The success of a decision is unpredictable,

And nervousness does not help the situation.

Never Judge a Book by its Cover

Anxiety will envelop your skin,
As you creep towards the unknown.
Sweat will pour down your visage,
As you creep towards the unknown.
Mystery will allure every cell in your body,
As you try to contemplate the possible outcomes.
The blood rushing within,
You judge, you scream, you avoid, you ignore.
And all this for what?
Experience the event first,
Then give your insightful thoughts!
Never judge a book by its cover,
And put to rest all the exaggerated rumours.

Let ecstasy encompass you,
Let joy overwhelm you.
Let surprise exhilarate you,
Let suspense mystify you.

These emotions are incomprehensible,
And we can only experience them,
If we stop judging a book by its cover.

The Power to Kill One's Passion

Ruthless and cruel are the words that describe this action,
This action which results in bluntness and boredom.
Personal motives are the reason behind this cruel action!

The cause burns bright within the fiery heart of the culprit,
Taking away the victim's passions!
Sucking the life out of everything he adores.
Making a hobby an agenda,
That is not the way we work today!
This is not what we do today!

The greed makes the culprit no better than a merciless spirit,
For he is the devil,
For taking away my passion!

Just a Smile

Smile from deep within till your heart's content,
Simply do it all the way with the right intent.
It only helps brighten your gloomy and forlorn day,
The satisfaction given is always there to stay.

With all the anxiety that constantly surrounds us,
Take a pause and try to wash away the crazy buzz.
A smile is priceless, it glitters flawlessly like gold,
Time and again in life's race we are inevitably under control.

Request yourself to break free and leave the unnecessary worries behind,
Take the time to consistently try and genuinely unwind.
Smile is infectious, it is nothing but solitude,
All we have to do is quantify and feel its real magnitude.

Spread its beautifully written story around,
With the help of thee you'll assertively stand back on the ground.
Smile only for yourself and none other,
Treat life like a palette of multiple
luminous colours.

Smile is contentment, it is simplicity,
Remember to engrave it on your face for all the world to bestow is not the right word here see.

Never Quit

When things go wrong, as they sometimes will,
When the road you stumble upon seems all uphill,
When pockets are empty and the debts are high,
And you deeply wish to smile, but you have to sigh.
When care is pushing you down a bit,
Do rest, if you must, but don't you dare quit.

Life is queer, with its twists and turns,
As each one of us at some point has to learn.
And many failures suddenly turn about,
When he might have won, had he stuck it out.
Don't ever give up though the pace seems terribly slow,
You will assertively succeed after another blow.

Success is nothing but a failure turned inside out,
It's a beautiful silver tint in the hopeless cloud of doubt.
You never can imagine how close you are,
But in reality, it is a short distance away when it seems so far.
Just strongly fight when you are hardest hit,
When things around seem at its worst,
That's when you must never quit.

Away

I was brought here, to my dream school,
This mystical wonderland of doubt.
I was away, far away from all that I knew,
The people I had heard of here were very few.

The days just go by,
Without hearing my family's his!
The enclosed space which I now call my new cozy home,
It is nothing more than a gleaming luminescent dome.

Now for weeks and weeks, I am stranded here,
With the slightest of knowledge and an abundance of fear.
For when will I grace my beloved with my presence?
I think I'm now working diligently, like a learning peasant.

Anxiety often grips my heart,
For my family and me are so far apart.
However, this is the righteous path for each one of us to take,
To finally leave our nest and get things done our way.

The number of years simply don't matter to me now,
For all the great heights I am able to reach and take a humble bow.
The independent me has finally risen with a sigh,
For I wish to fly high up, deep into the extensive sky.
I hear an aggressive internal debate with the real me,
As long as I am as free as one can be.

Blue

As I dived,
I divided into infinity almost a world untold.
Literally like an unexplored planet,
Another universe.

At first I saw nothing—nothing that was unnerving,
Bubbles and only bubbles—escaping from my regulator as they innocently floated to the smooth surface.

Utmost tranquility was the feeling I experienced on watching them float up,
As I descended slowly but steadily,
life under became more and more interesting.

In the distant bottom stood a rock—a humongous rock.
This 'rock' supported the most mesmerizing reef.
The exuberant colours struck my naked eyes,
And I was transfixed all of a sudden.

There was an adrenaline rush and then all that remained was ecstasy!
The endless blue all around me was ignored at once as I dived towards the hidden life that dwelled below.

A million colourful fish caught my sight,
The school displayed a bright silver pattern that seemed to hypnotize me.
Unfortunately, their joy was short-lived for there came the ferocious and cunning sharks.

Eight was the number!
They circled around and tactically broke them up,
Those cavernous mouths engulfed hundreds at a time!

And at the sad end, there were almost none left,
Just like the words in my mouth have suddenly vanished
to describe what I had just seen.
Leaving me speechless,
the gigantic blue has a life,
A life quite different from what lies above.

Eternally Strive

The wildebeest lay ahead, above the adolescent plateau,
An immeasurable distance away lay a ferocious lion.
The beast with his tanned skin and honoured presence,
With his glorious yet fluffy mane and the status—
that of Caesar himself.

But will this Caesar too be killed by his beloved Brutus, the one he would die for?
The lion lunged and galloped towards the beast, with arms stiff and mouth poised to sink in,
But alas, the plateau was far too grand, the statue of Colossus you could call it.

However, the lion endured, endlessly striving up the gritty yet untouched wonder of nature's architecture,
For he was nearly there.
As he reached the peak, the horizon came into view,
The tranquility and serenity of the view was far too picturesque for the lion to continue his pursuit.

The wildebeest escaped in time but the starved lion did not care,
For he just proudly stood on the rock,
That overlooked his kingdom.
He just stood there, the drowning sun disappearing against his fearsome eyes.

Almost like he had swallowed it with a loud, echoing ear-shattering sound escaping his throat,
The roar of great success and triumph.
For even though he did not achieve his goal,
The journey was worth the mystical view.

The Long Walk

I exit the pale wooden door,
I walk.
I silently stop,
Looking down at the soft silky snow beneath my feet.

I walk,
I gaze around.
I see the frigid stream gushing beside me.
I walk
past the great
white dome on my right.

I walk,
I walk over the antique bridge that was carved from a
gigantic stone.
I walk,
I walk right under the gallows where the hangman stayed.

I walk,
I walk right between the trees
that protrude from the soil beneath.
I walk,
I walk right up that steep mountain
that lies right in front of me.

I walk,
I ascend with one heavy step
after another, gasping for breath.

I walk,
I walk right to the peak,
Feeling like a king on his throne or a great achiever.

I walk,
I walk the long walk.
I walk all day—never to stop!

What?

Everything around is a vivid blur of green, amber and magenta,
Light is travelling as if it were a sloth right before my very observant eyes.

The acrid smell that was external,
Unpleasantly and unwelcomingly enters through my sore nose,
I hear echoes and faint screeches like cries of help and lost voices drowning in the eternal pool of the unknown.

I can taste it, repulsively yet serenely it dissolves in the jelly-like pores of my tongue until it is devoured forever,
I can feel the craggy surface with my bare skin.

It pricks me, yet I hold it,
It divulges into a smooth velvety cover that I wear and will only discard once I don't need it.
This is much more than I can handle and yet something which is an innate part of us.

The Outsider

There I stood on the precipice,
Knowing this was the end.
Discomposed as I was,
I realized that it had come to this.
I was merely an outsider,
With no real connection to this world.
With no real interaction with this world,
I was merely an outsider.

My toes stretched beyond the solid ground,
As I took a few steps forward.
My head was in line with the ocean,
I could feel the tranquil breeze
brushing against my face.
I was merely an outsider,
Standing alone on this desolate island.
Standing alone as I always had,
I was merely an outsider.

I put my hands by my side,
Prepared to make the leap.
Trembling with boundless fear,
I knew this was the end.
I was merely an outsider,
Waiting for someone who never arrived.
Waiting a lifetime for emptiness to approach,
I was merely an outsider.

Sweat trickled down my creased head,
My brows furrowed as if holding on to each other for support,
My nose grew stiff and my ears were turned out.
I was merely an outsider,
Being tuned out my entire life.
Being frowned upon as I made my way forward,
I was merely an outsider.

I slowly stopped,
Motionless, I sensed tranquility.
Motionless, I watched the picturesque coast,
I slowly turned and paced back.
Sure, I was merely an outsider,
But maybe that's what made me stand out!
That's what made me who I am today!
I am merely an outsider.

The Power of Letting Go

To let go does not mean that I've stopped caring,
It simply means I am tired and can't do it anymore.
To let go is not to cut myself off from the world around,
It's the realization that I can't control another.

To let go is not to enable,
But to allow important learnings from natural consequences.
To let go is to admit powerlessness,
Which in turn means that the outcome is beyond my control.

To let go is not to try and change or blame another,
It is because the real change is only within me.
To let go is not to care for—but to care about,
To let go is not to fix—but to be supportive.

To let go is not to be judgemental,
It's the ultimate freedom to let everyone simply be.
To let go is not to be the mediator arranging the eventualities,
But to allow others to face their own outcomes bravely.

To let go is not to be protective,
But to permit one another to face the harsh reality,
To let go is not to deny—but to accept.
To let go is not to squabble or argue,
But to identify one's shortcomings with utmost humility.

To let go is not to expect everything as I desire,
But to take each day as it comes and cherish the moment.

To let go is not to criticize and regulate another,
But to try and become more accepting.

To let go is not to regret the past,
But to grow maturely in the present and live for the future.
To let go is to fear less,
And instead learn to love more.

Snowflake

Bound together, bound forever,
Let their bond never sever.
For they are transcendent,
With an everlasting crystalline connection,
Displaying numerous sections.

For they are bound together,
By the great gaseous giant floating above.
Seems almost impossible that they would ever separate!
Is it chance or is it fate?

The roar of the mighty crackled down,
As the great gaseous giant has lost its crown.
And alas! The translucent flake falls,
Falls, away from everything.

As he is entering the world of reality,
He loses all his friends,
He loses everyone.

Yet, he descends,
Still he falls.
The silky soft touch,
The slight sparkle of the flake.

It's all evident now as he evolves,
Evolves into a greater self.
This journey he has embarked upon,
Leaves him alone.
Yet he continues to fall,
And he falls right into his vibrant future!

Wait

Wait! Take a deep soothing and satisfying breath,
It's time to reduce your pace as the world around us is nothing but an endless race.
We have forgotten the pure essence of the enchantress,
The fascinating vision of the picturesque horizon right in front.

Wait! Please slow down and pause for a while,
If not, our lives will be nothing but in exile.
Let us cherish all the small and big exciting adventures experienced so far,
For we seldom realize the priceless value of an entire era.

Wait! Appreciate your loved ones like never before,
There is more to life than simply doing your taxing chores.
While working tirelessly, don't forget to observe the wilderness and calm around,
For the race we are a part of simply tends to go round and round.

Wait! Just for this one last time, after all the running,
For before it's too late we must realize the significance of every single thing.
After a never-ending war between peace and rumble,
It's the egoistic rumble that eventually surrenders.

Wait! Time is running out but we need to take a conscious step back just to unwind,
For love and happiness are the real achievements at the bottom of every single line.

Why mourn after death,
It is nothing but a mirror that makes us reflect on every lost breath.
Wait! Let's start slow and steady,
Only to finally acknowledge, learn and magnify all that's here and ready.

Into the Wild

I eagerly watched,
Watched the fine golden rays at dusk,
Highlighting the tall erect trees and grasslands.
A sudden excitement, a sudden hustle struck the enchanted,
Everything came alive, so pure and divine,
The breathtaking nature felt increasingly sublime.

A variety of alluring birds lit up the gigantic blue sky,
Completely mesmerizing every passer-by.
Like the pristine beauty of a virgin untouched and untold,
It's for us to cherish and strongly hold.
I eagerly watched!

Watched the roaring fight for power and hunger,
The circle of life sometimes makes me want to wonder.
A life so dissimilar to ours—no limits, no boundaries, only freedom filled in the air,
This lesson is simple, but most of us are absolutely unaware.

There comes the mighty king with his pride,
Portraying a sense of sudden discipline so precise.
I eagerly watched!

Watched the time pass by gracefully from dusk to dawn,
With everything changing slowly but steadily like life in a spawn.
After this came a sudden deep darkness,
A darkness so uncertain, so infinite,
Impatiently waiting to engulf the underdogs.

Those sparkling fearless eyes playing hide and seek,
At once, the mighty nocturnal world was at its peak.
I eagerly watched!
Watched the scuffle without a perfect vision,
For the wild is something that I cannot fathom.

Figure it Out

Drip, drip,
Drop, drop,
Out comes that luminescent drop.
Drips down excitedly from the now faded cloud
glowing under the sun.
Its translucent beauty so visible,
A spray of colours shooting out,
Just as the multiple rays divulge within.

The drops gather to form a puddle,
A sudden unity flourishing, they bond and stay strong.
Until separated by the greater body they call...
God!
He breaks them apart for pure fun,
An easy task it appears to be,
Something for our leisure,
A regular task it appears to be.

The drops never reunite,
But form new groups, new puddles,
Mixing and meeting,
Until there are none of them left.

The sun so powerful and strong,
Appears similar to a runny yolk of a fresh egg,
It literally makes them vanish until there are no more left.

And so the cycle continues...

Time

Oh time! Please pause for a while,
Just to embrace and to feel.
Why are you always in a haste?
For you are someone who doesn't wish to wait.

Decades go by, experiencing euphoria and often despair,
Cherish each and every moment as you never know what's about to appear ahead.
Everything being a question mark,
Just to get the right answer we impatiently wait for,
As in a lifetime, we watch generations grow from young to old.

Oh time! Please stop for a while,
Just to hold and to cherish.
Why are you a complete wreck?
For you…you limitlessly bind us all.
With your speed and rigid discipline,
None can escape or crawl.

You being in perpetual control,
The anxiety within tends to take a toll.
Poor you! You bear the burden of witnessing constant highs and lows,
For you are someone who stands upright to always bear the blow.

Oh time! Please pause for a while,
Just to sing and to rejoice.

Why don't you try and look back?
With you, everything seems to simply pass by.

A jittery feeling surrounds us all,
As soon as the bad times are all set to bawl.
You are our greatest teacher, a guide and a soulmate in many ways,
With all due respect it's time you bow down to our pace.

Oh time! Please pause for a while,
Just to watch and to see.
Why do you wish to fly?
For with you, life seems to only magnify.

Witnessing all the different eras,
Filled with anger, anguish, agony one after another.
Why? Is it so hard to live in harmony with each other?
We should remember and embrace,
Let's overlook the bad and focus on the good instead.

Oh time! Please pause for a while,
Just to nurture and to care.
Why don't you realize what's at stake?
It's time you slow down for us to value and celebrate.

Dream

So near yet so far,
I dare, dare to dream with all my power.
A duplicate life—a life I live in the wee hours,
Seldom feeling lonely,
Just laying still, although experiencing an exciting thrill.

So real, yet such a sham,
I dare, dare to dream with all my might.
With shivers down my wretched spine, nervousness strikes,
Hope you understand my never-ending plight.

So cold yet so torrid, I dare,
Dare to dream with a face so fearlessly horrid.
Engulfed with varied emotions,
Oh help! Please pull me out of this terrible commotion.

So dear, yet so despised, I dare,
Dare to dream with an intelligent disguise.
Just like watching an unknown movie,
Right from the beginning until the end—feeling groovy.

So swift yet so steady, I dare,
Dare to dream with an anxious heart,
About an experience so superficially enthralling.
At the wake of dawn,
Finally, the time has come to put an end to this insane plan.

The Soulful Woman

After a prolonged anxious wait,
There comes a melodious beautiful cry.
Silken hair playing constant hide and seek with her delicate face,
Wiggling her tiny fingers and toes.

A first, there is a starry look, all confused and ready to doze,
Numerous questions forming within.
Selfless love and excitement fills the air,
Growing up innocently not knowing
what lies in her journey ahead.

Transitioning all the way from her little shy self to adolescence,
Now burdened with numerous responsibilities.
Will there ever be an end?
Or will it simply multiply and kill all her radiant dreams.

It's time to applaud and respect her identity,
As she alone bears it all, without a complaint or a frown.
This bubble will burst when the picture is crystal
clear all around,
She will finally breathe—breathe a sigh of relief.

In a world which is safe and surrounded by nothing but peace,
Her sacrifice is larger than life.
It's time to pause and give her a huge bow,
For if it wasn't for her we would all be surrounded with
nothing but doubt.

A mother, a sister, a wife, a daughter,
She plays all the powerful roles with utmost perfection and grace.
Then why do we trouble her from time to time—giving a life filled with continuous denial?

Let realization strike—a heart filled with gratitude and beaming pride.
Our existence is solely in her pure hands,
For she alone is none other than the woman of substance we have all known.
And after all the introspection,
I must admit that I am her greatest fan.

Gratitude Concealed

The world around us, shining like luminous gold,
But the feelings within are often untold.
A persistent burden that crowds our thoughts,
We often feel miserably lost.
Let's come together and show some genuine gratitude,
And consciously work on changing our rigid attitude.

The air we breathe is always in abundance,
But we seldom realize its absolute significance.
We must fill our hearts with utmost peace and contentment,
As positivity to others we seldom lend.
Let's come together and show some genuine gratitude,
For then will we understand its sheer magnitude.

The love and happiness we feel is only pure,
But the debate within keeps us hungry for more.
It is time to acknowledge this gifted life,
To challenge ourselves and to strive.
Let's come together and show some genuine gratitude,
As only then will there be an end to this unnecessary feud.

My Melodious Guitar

Her strings were soft and smooth as silk,
Encompassed within her ever so sturdy frame.
All natural, I would assume,
For out of her, did emerge,
An everlasting melodious tune.

I placed her on my lap gently,
My fingers ran down her frail body.
I looked at her, admiring god's impeccable creation,
She stared at me—a relentless stare.
She wanted me, she wanted my smooth fingers,
Against her thin and fragile strings.
For there was a hollow in her,
A hollow, only I could fill with the gracious octave,
A hollow that could only be filled with music and symphony.

I stroked her,
My fingers ran down her tense strings.
For I was the saviour,
For she did feel the jingle,
And glee enveloped her surface.
For she knew she was safe,
In my tireless arms,
My companion—my melodious guitar!

My Treasured Grandmother

Grandma, oh my beloved Grandma!
Deep loneliness fills my aching heart,
I find it challenging to make a fresh start.
You are there in my fondest memories,
As tough as you were, you made me defeat all my worries.

Grandma, oh my beloved Grandma!
I am left in pain as I miss you so very much,
What in this world I wouldn't do,
Just to feel your magical touch.
You always taught me how to be me,
I have to admit, that made me feel so free.

Grandma, oh my beloved Grandma!
With your thoughts, my eyes drip with sadness and tears,
Now left deserted, there is none who can help me face my fears.
My love and reverence for you cannot be measured,
Your adoration and blessings will always be treasured.

Grandma, oh my beloved Grandma!
Why, oh why, did you leave me in so much pain,
For, it being the Almighty's wish,
There is no one to blame.
I may not be there in person in your resting place,

But I shower all my respect, fondness and homage to you in pure grace.

I love and miss you more than words can ever express,
And I just want to say—you are one in a million.

In Vain

After the gloomy darkness comes a luminous bright light,
Then why do we indulge in this ugly fight?
Let us simply look and see,
How everything around has gotten so poor and deceased.

Is it what we really want?
Or is it jealousy and the mighty ego,
Rumbling against each other to win this war.
Love is simply forgotten—like those good old days,
It's hatred that's come out strong by making an enormous gain.

Happiness, are you lost somewhere,
In this world which is getting ready to blare?
It's this scrupulous game of hide and seek being played all along,
By no one, for we do not know what to really hide and
where to seek.

Wake up before it is too late,
Stop this rumble and have utmost faith.
A faith to turn things around,
A faith to come back to the ground.
Let's stand up united to overcome this struggle,
For only love and happiness surrounds us all.

It's in our hands to choose the right from wrong,
Then tell me, why do we choose to be in vain?

Mystical Tree

From being a tiny little seed,
You have taken a long journey indeed.
Years of hard work and compassion,
The outcome so gracefully portrayed
in all dimensions.

A seed, a sprout—a sapling,
Soon gaining full maturity and entering confidently
into adulthood.
Spreading yourself wide,
Standing tall, erect and strong,
Giving life and freshness all along.

Tell me, are you feeling anxious or tired?
For without your support,
We would all be eternally dead.
Blossoming with vibrant shades
From time to time,
A sight so pure and sublime.

You are home to numerous beings,
A sense of calm and peace exists,
Standing right beneath.
You serve, serve like no other,
Selflessly standing alone, devoted forever.
A never-ending task with days, months and years flying by,
Tell me, are you feeling sad or lonely?
I am always there to give you a big pat on your back.

All ready to help and save you from the ruthlessness around,
Coming together to bow in front of you with utmost gratitude.
Care and comfort given by you secures one and all,
Oh! My beautiful mystical tree, now it is time to give you a round of applause.

A Beautiful Day

After a dark night, finally strikes the dawn,
Slowly yet cautiously rising up,
There comes the magical flaming ball.
Shy and timid at first,
Peeking out of its horizon,
Consistently with every passing season.

Blazing the clear blue sky with vivid shades of warmth,
Just like a symphony of mother nature,
So creatively put together.
Shining brighter as time ticks by,
Giving life and glamour all along the way.

It's a wonder beyond imagination,
A mastermind filled with intense passion.
Always at the centre, guiding like an enlightened guru,
Never fails or falters as a common man,
For our existence is purely in its hands.

After a long and tiresome journey,
Perspiring profusely surrounded in flames,
Selflessly working hard with no personal gain.

It is time to lay low now with the dusk coming on strong,
Cooling and slowing down all underneath with a view
simply mesmerizing.
Mighty darkness wraps itself around so tight,
Keeps us anxiously waiting for the next beautiful day to arrive.

The Road Ahead

Standing under the scorching sun,
Waiting to overcome my deadly emotions.
Why is the road ahead so long and wretched,
Is it trying hard to teach me life's glorified lessons?

I pause to look back and see what I've left behind,
All the way till my eyes reach, I witness sheer silence,
which portrays calmness indeed.
I hold my breath to peacefully think of what lies ahead,
Is it the beautiful life or the mighty death?

Death is just a new beginning for us to stumble upon,
Life is nothing but filled with solitude all along.
I choose life over death for there is much left to explore,
A journey which my heart eagerly waits to undertake.

I silently walk my path filled with excitement,
Simply weaving away everlasting memories to stay.
I know the road ahead may not be smooth and straight,
Maybe with some sudden bumps that are in your fate.

The fearless me is now ready to explore the rare,
Similar to a game of truth and dare.
It's a journey full of greatest adventures unseen,
For us to cherish and endeavour thee.

The road ahead,
Filled with knowledge and awareness,

A tool so powerful like words seldom spoken.
Self-realization strikes me hard,
As wisdom I am awaiting to impart.

Beauty lies in the eyes of the beholder they say,
It's the greatest education along the way,
With my vision blurred,
I am trying to find the way through the dark.

The road ahead
makes me experience and cherish the untold and the unheard,
Waiting to embark.

The Great Artist

Unlimited colours on nature's vast palette,
Filled with warmth all the way.
Blending in so effortlessly,
And yet so effectively.

Keep looking with those sparkling eyes,
For something spectacular is sure to arise,
A task enriching and yet satisfying.
Hues produced are unimaginable,
For the great artist is supremely capable.

Everything around is vibrant yet surreal,
Stand still and enjoy this mystical experience.
Show love and admiration towards it with all your heart,
For you never know when time will take you apart.

Everything around is picture perfect,
Endless lines and forms defining it beautifully.
I wish to hold a brush and add beauty to this picturesque painting,
Simply to preserve what the great artist has bestowed upon us.
I wish to bow down and appreciate all his enormous efforts,
For there can never be another.

Printed in the USA
CPSIA information can be obtained
at www.ICGtesting.com
LVHW091400140824
788218LV00001B/47